PARENTING

OUR YOUNG ADULTS WITH

LOVE & BACKBONE

The Practice Of Supportive Integrity

Jack Stoltzfus, PhD

Parenting Our Young Adults with Love and Backbone: The Practice of Supportive Integrity

This is the fifth in a series of books on parental practices that help support the young adult's task of independence.

Can You Speak Millennial "ese"? How to Understand and Communicate with Your Young Adult
Love to Let Go: Loving Our Kids into Adulthood
Apology: The Gift We Give Our Young Adults
Forgiveness: The Gift We Share with Our Young Adults and Ourselves
Parenting Our Young Adults with Love and Backbone: The Practice of Supportive Integrity
Growing Apart: Letting Go of Our Young Adults

Books are available at www.parentslettinggo.com and www.Amazon.com.

ISBN 978-0-9985543-4-1

Dr. Jack Stoltzfus
www.parentslettinggo.com

Contents

Preface

Parents who attend my Parents Letting Go workshops or read this book and the other practice books in the series do so because they are facing a challenging situation with their young adults and want answers. I spent five minutes making a list of the many challenging situations or problems parents of young adults face. When I was done I had come up with more than one hundred situations. In this series on parents letting go, previous practice books have provided guidance on foundational practices parents need to strengthen (understanding and unconditional love) and healing practices (apology and forgiveness). These prerequisite practices are essential to building the type of relationship where parents can have influence, set limits, and be respected. All the books are available at www.parentslettinggo.com and www. Amazon.com.

Over the last thirty years I have worked as a psychologist with adolescents and young adults and their parents to help facilitate the natural launching process that has become complicated and problematic. Complicating factors range from a foreboding threat of suicide to the more mundane problem of getting the young adult to be less of a video-game-playing couch potato. The most common feeling expressed by parents at my workshops has been "frustration." This often speaks to the sense of helplessness they feel to motivate or influence their young adult in what they view as constructive. As a parent of three young adults, my wife and I have been challenged to determine when do we help and when do we say no.

This is **not** a book to address all of the one hundred specific issues on my list. Rather, the goal is to provide general principles and guidelines that parents can follow that speak to the need to be understanding, loving, forgiving, and compassionate while exhibiting *backbone*—the ability to say "no." In most cases guidelines and principles are followed by applications and examples.

Being a parent of a young adult is more challenging than at any other time in history, yet parents of young adults are often ignored with a view that their job is done, so education and resources are often in short supply. This book will help you learn why, how, and when to stand your ground and set limits that will enable your young adult to move toward responsible independence.

Note: The last two books in the practice series are focused on defining the relationship between parents and young adults. *Parenting Our Young Adults With Love and Backbone* involves establishing clear delineation and boundaries between the parent and young adult that set the stage for letting go. *Growing Apart* describes a new relationship with new roles, boundaries, and expectations as both parties move on with their lives.

About the Author

Dr. Jack Stoltzfus is a licensed psychologist practicing in Shoreview, Minnesota. He
received his PhD in counseling psychology
from the University of Wisconsin-Madison
and is a member of the American Psychological Association. The focus of his PhD
dissertation was on defining and measuring
healthy adolescent separation from parents.
His private practice is focused on parents
and young adults. Dr. Stoltzfus has worked
with parents and their young adult children within the context of a
chemical dependency day treatment program, inpatient mental health
facilities, a child guidance clinic, a youth service agency, and a private
practice for more than thirty years. He has practiced family therapy as
a Certified Marriage and Family Therapist and substance abuse counseling as a Licensed Alcohol and Drug Counselor. He has three grown
and married young adult children who represent the millennial and
early Gen X generations.

Dr. Stoltzfus has developed and launched the website parentslet-
tinggo.com to educate and support parents on practices or actions
they can take to support a healthy launch of their young adult children. Visit the website to access this book as well as the five other
"practice" publications and other resources. The information is provided for parents of young adults who have been a neglected segment
of the population in research and writing and yet want answers and
guidance more than any other generation of parents.

What Would You Do?

- A twenty-three-year-old college graduate is content with staying at home and staying up late at night playing video games and refuses to take a job that is not in his field of study.

- A young adult who is angry with his parents for not allowing him to use the car takes a martial arts weapon—a ball with sharp edges on a chain—and rakes the house and furniture.

- A twenty-four-year-old male with a severe alcohol problem and several stints in a treatment program asks to live at home because he cannot keep a job.

- A twenty-five-year-old college graduate working as personal trainer causes her parents to worry and wonder when she will get a real job.

- A twenty-five-year-old with Asperger's and ADHD is fearful of moving out on his own, and his parents share this concern but want him to be independent.

- A female single parent of two children who is struggling to make ends meet, with an ex-husband who fails to provide child support, asks her parents for financial help with nursing school so she can get a better job.

- A single parent young adult asks his mother for money to pay legal fees for his custody battle over his son.

This last situation, you may be surprised to learn, involves a fifty-nine-year-old son who recently fathered a child and made the request of his ninety-five-year-old mother. For better or worse, we are all parents for life. Although this last situation is clearly unique, they all are ones I have faced in my private practice. Many of you may have similar situations and want to "cut to the chase" and get the answer to the question raised above. And I promise you I will provide some guidance, if not some specific advice, but first it's important to lay the groundwork for how to address these types of situations.

CHAPTER 1

How Do I Begin to Show Love and Backbone?

Some foundational work needs to be done by parents to be successful with the launching task. It begins by having a mindset based upon certain critical assumptions and then subscribing to the key practices that facilitate the letting go process.

All practices are predicated on accepting certain **basic assumptions** about young adults and our response to them. As parents we:

1. Cannot control our young adults.

2. Are not responsible for their decisions, actions and feelings.

3. Are responsible for our decisions, actions and feelings.

4. Will not use the past to excuse their actions or ours.

5. Need to balance love (support) and emancipation (letting go).

6. Understand relationships are inherently reciprocal—how we treat our young adult children will determine how they treat us.

7. Believe change starts with us—thinking, behaving, and feeling differently.

If you have trouble subscribing to one or more of these assumptions, it may become difficult to follow the guidance offered around the practice of supportive integrity. Here are two additional assumptions that relate to this practice.

8. Integrity is something parents must exhibit and children, including young adults, expect.

9. Saying no and taking a stand in support of integrity is not unloving. It may be the most loving and empowering statement we can make to our young adult.

No is not a four-letter word

A few comments about the two additional assumptions: From the beginning of their role, parents are tasked with teaching values—right from wrong, honesty, keeping promises, being fair, being responsible, and so forth. These should not change when a child becomes an adolescent or young adult. With young adults, parents may have to revisit the question of what is the right thing to do relative to their values and not what feels good.

From early on, one of the first words a toddler learns is no. Often they overlearn this and turn it back on us as parents, pushing a food away that they don't like and saying no. When we say no to toddling into the street, picking up a knife, or touching the hot burner on the stove, we are exhibiting integrity.

When children become adolescents and young adults, we must continue to exhibit integrity by saying no to their actions that are unsafe, destructive, illegal, or irresponsible. The difference is that we rarely can stop or intervene as we did with a young child (see assumption number one listed previously). Even though the young adult protests vehemently, we have to remain firm in what we believe.

The measure of what we do should be our values and what we believe as parents is the right thing to do, not the reaction of the young adult or what makes us feel better. There is one caveat to this last point: The values we hold as parents and apply to the young adult should be consistent with general community standards. Harming or threatening to harm the young adult if he or she does not do what you want would not be consistent with common young adult parenting practices. As parents, if we have tended to give in on many occasions because we don't want the young adult to be unhappy or reject us, resetting the relationship based upon integrity will be difficult and resisted. But read on.

Letting Go Practices of Parents

The focus of this book, as illustrated in the diagram above, is on supportive integrity. But successfully launching a young adult into mature independence isn't a function of only one practice. In fact, if the other practices leading up to this one are not demonstrated or strengthened, this practice will be more challenging if not impossible. If you have not spent time listening and trying to understand your young adult, expressing unconditional love, owning your failures and shortcomings, and practicing forgiveness, your efforts to exhibit integrity may be resisted.

For example, if your young adult does not believe that they are loved, their reactivity to your setting limits or boundaries may be misplaced. I discussed the situation involving my father and my belief that he did not love or accept me as a source of my anger and reactivity in an earlier practice book, *Love to Let Go: Loving Our Kids into Adulthood* (see www.parentslettinggo.com).

Another example is a young adult who is holding onto anger and resentment about some neglect or abuse experienced from you in early years. If this is the case, the young adult is going to be less open to your influence or setting limits until you step up with an apology. Not every parent needs to strengthen every practice, but if you and your young adult are struggling with the launch process and there is a lot of emotion and reactivity on either your part or theirs, revisiting the first four practices may provide some insight. At www.parentslettinggo.com and through the other practice books, you can take quizzes that will enable you to gauge how well you are doing with the other practices.

CHAPTER 2

What Do Integrity and Backbone Mean?

Integrity is the clear and demonstrated principles, values, and ethics that govern life and relationships. Integrity includes:

- Honesty, fairness, and openness.

- Clear and strong moral and ethical principles.

- Words and actions that match principles.

- Willingness to take a stand on principles and show backbone.

- Willingness to bear the consequences of taking a stand.

The Josephson Institute summarizes integrity as "the moral commitment and courage necessary to maintain consistency between what we believe, what we say, what we do, and what we are morally obligated to do."[1]

Values of Integrity

1. The commitment of parents to be consistent in applying their values and principles is important to teaching children—young or old—how to effectively approach life and relationships. We can't expect the schools or even the churches to do this. It's our job, and it doesn't end at the young adult stage. We may not be able to

impose particular values on young adults, but we should not back away from modeling and communicating them.

2. Young adults need a solid foundation on which they can define and differentiate themselves. If parents are wishy-washy and inconsistent, the young adult learns that integrity doesn't matter. Although not a given, many teens and young adults differentiate themselves by asserting their differences with their parents. This is normal and not a bad thing unless asserting themselves involves harmful or illegal actions. Parents may need to allow for differences in things such as dress, music, Xbox games, and friends, but need to stay firm on honesty, responsibility, safety, and other big issues.

3. If we don't hold the line with expectations regarding appropriate behavior and follow through with consequences when our children are growing up, we will end up defaulting to society to do this. In my practice I have worked with families where the adolescent is out of control and his or her illegal actions result in the courts taking over control. If we can teach cause and effect and consequences for actions during childhood, young adults are less likely to have to experience this from the justice system. That said, I have worked with very loving and firm parents whose adolescent/young adult has chosen a path of self-destruction that the parents were not able to change. We have to remind ourselves of these assumptions: We can't control our young adults and we aren't responsible for their actions.

> *There is no harder truth for a parent to bear . . .*
> *and it is this: love is not enough.*
> —Sue Klebold

Supportive Integrity

"Supportive" integrity incorporates the aspects of love, caring, and nurturance with the harder side of integrity. Standing firm without incorporating love for the young adult will often engender antagonism and resistance, which will be discussed later in the book. "Tough love," when defined correctly, really represents this combination of unconditional love for the young adult with love and firmness on parental principles—**backbone**.

Being firm and being loving are not mutually exclusive.

CHAPTER 3

What Qualities Are Important to Supportive Integrity?

Show integrity, backbone, and fortitude. Take a minute to look up the definitions of these words and ask yourself how much you demonstrate these

qualities. Being a parent isn't a popularity contest. At times you must make the hard decisions that involve saying no, expressing disapproval or standing behind consequences that you or others have set. You owe it to yourself and your young adult not to be a wimp or a doormat. Be someone they know who has a bottom line, a limit, and certain, clear values that are solid and unmovable. Remember the foundational assumptions: You are not responsible for their actions—you are responsible for yours. Also, taking a stand is something parents must do and children expect, and it is not unloving.

Grow a backbone! Say what you mean and mean what you say.

Communicate and model values, standards, and principles you want your child to learn. Young adults are quick to spot hypocrisy and call parents on it. They have a great BS scanner. It's important to ask yourself: How consistent am I with my young adult? With the young adult's siblings? With people outside the family?

Do you walk the talk?

Be transparent, honest, and open in facing challenges to your integrity. Allow them to see that you don't have all of the answers and that you are trying to figure out how to be a parent of a young adult as much as they are trying to figure out how to be a young adult with you. Honesty as a quality or value is foundational to any relationship. It is even more important than love, although you clearly need both. Without honesty there is no trust, and love can't survive. Also be willing to be open to reflecting and revising your values. We need to recognize that our young adult's values may be different than ours. Be willing to negotiate and compromise in seeking a more collegial relationship versus one based on a power imbalance. Rigidity often triggers resistance in the young adult. This is a period of moving from control and being right to one of shared power and decision-making, and the identification of solutions.

Be real, be honest, and be open to change. No one, including parents, has a lock on the truth.

Demonstrate empathy and compassion through listening and tuning in to their needs. Empathy involves stepping into their shoes. It involves reconnecting with your own young adulthood and trying to understand their experience, which may be similar or different than yours. Sharing your own young adult experience, particularly if it was difficult, can affirm your young adult's experience. Compassion is an ability to identify with the suffering of another and a desire to help them eliminate this suffering.

True listening to your young adult involves a heartfelt connection to their needs and desires.

Develop the capacity to understand and consider your young adult's needs for identity, independence, and intimacy. This is one of the toughest times in a person's development. These are such big tasks to face. We often have selective memory about our own experience and forget some of the difficulties we had at this stage. If we listen closely with empathy and compassion, we will penetrate the walls of resistance we might experience with the young adult and connect to their hopes and fears related to one or more of these tasks.

A good question for parents to ask when trying to understand and connect to the young adult is: What developmental task are they facing?

Be courageous and admit mistakes, apologize, forgive, and learn from your young adult. Such actions are demonstrations of integrity and invite similar responses from the young adult; one of the basic assumptions is that relationships are inherently reciprocal. We don't have all of the answers and aren't always right. In this time of rapid change and advances in technology, our young adults are often more knowledgeable than us in certain things. Being willing to ask and seek advice shows you don't have all of the answers. For those of us who are digital immigrants, we depend on our children to set up and fix our electronic devices or to help us understand social media and the impact it has on their lives. When we ask them for help or advice, they are more likely to be open to our help and advice.

It's important to acknowledge that we make mistakes, are trying to do the right thing as parents, and are still learning.

Practice balance in your view and observations of your young adult. There is quite a bit of evidence that these young adults share much of the conventional values we may hold, such as gainful employment, marriage, and children. We need to pay as much attention to signals of these types of values as we do to signs that they are not demonstrating our desired values. Too often parents are looking for the problem or concern and quick to point this out. A good rule of thumb is to express positive observations and comments about the young adult's behavior at a ratio of four to one related to negative or critical comments.

Catch and affirm the young adult's demonstration of positive values and behaviors.

CHAPTER 4

Do I Have Integrity?

Difficulty Maintaining Integrity: Quiz

A definition of the word *backbone* is a "firm and resolute character."[2] We all know the word and likely use it at times, particularly in instances when we think our young adults are not standing up for themselves or for their values. But having a backbone, a firm and resolute character, is easier said than done. Some parents really struggle with being firm. The following self-assessment will help you identify actions that suggest you are having trouble exhibiting backbone.

Below is a list of some actions that demonstrate one has difficulty maintaining integrity. To what extent do you exhibit these behaviors? Use the following scale and write your number in front of each statement.

0   1   2   3   4   5   6   7   8   9   10

Not at all   Completely

_____ A. Avoid bringing up an issue or concern because you fear your young adult's reaction.

_____ B. Doing things for your young adult that they could do for themselves.

_____ C. Support, excuse (they are stressed, depressed, forgot), or allow irresponsible behavior.

_____ D. Give in on a request that you know is not right according to your values.

_____ E. Intervene with people and institutions (school, work, doctor) on behalf of your young adult.

_____ F. Do things for your young adult primarily to make you feel better or less guilty.

_____ G. Tolerate verbal or physical abusive behavior.

_____ H. Blame others for the failures of the young adult and promote a victim mindset.

_____ I. Excuse behavior due to a condition or disability that does not prevent the young adult from performing the task.

_____ J. Ignore your own needs and self-care and overextend yourself on behalf of your young adult.

How did you score (a lower score is better)? Can you identify some actions that you need to change? Which two of your actions scored the highest? Check them on the list. Decide to address one or more of these in the "Call to Action" in chapter 10. There are many resources on enabling the type of behavior illustrated above; they are listed in the bibliography on page 80. Find one or more that interests you to understand and make changes in this behavior.

Why as parents do we fail to demonstrate backbone? There are many reasons we end up enabling irresponsible behavior and don't take the stand we need to. Here's a short list of some of these reasons. Do any of them explain one or more of your high scores above?

- Depend on our adult children to meet our need for approval and happiness.

- Fear that they may fail, get hurt, or make mistakes; this thinking leads to overprotection and undermining of independence.

- Feel guilty and can't say no to requests that are inconsistent with our values.

- Try to heal our childhood wounds. We were mistreated as children and want to make up for this with our young adults.

- Need to be pleasers, fixers, or doormats, always trying to make our young adults happy.

- Fear conflict and avoid or walk away rather than hold to our values.

- Want to be fair to a fault; our kids need to know life isn't always fair.

- Have a high need to be right or be in control.

Are there one or two of reasons above that you would like to change in your approach—either words or actions—to your young adult? Consider addressing these in the "Call to Action" section in chapter 10.

The risks of parental failure to demonstrate integrity can be summarized in five ways.

Parents who refuse to let go and continue to demonstrate a need to be right and in control at a time when the adolescent or young adult is striving for independence.

Parents who fall into roles of pleasers, caretakers, or enablers and avoid conflict and do everything in their power, including compromising their values, to please the young adult or avoid rejection.

Parents who exhibit a mixed approach, giving in at times and rigidly taking a strong stand at other times, sometimes on the same issue. This inconsistent approach, which has been demonstrated in research on parenting children, is often quite damaging to the relationship and influence the parent might have. This not only applies to inconsistency within one parent's approach but inconsistency between the parents. This is a common problem for parents where one takes a tough and sometimes harsh approach demanding that the young adult experience consequences and the other takes a softer, nurturing approach. The parents increase their preferred approach to counteract the other parent's approach, and they push each other to the extreme causing mixed messages for the young adult and recursive conflict between the parents. In some cases parents have actually ended their relationship over this and may even point to the young adult as the cause of their split. In reality, they failed to work as a team.

Parents who are meeting their own needs in hanging onto the young adult. These needs can be from the parent's childhood when the parent experienced neglect or trauma, or from guilt associated with some failure in raising the young adult or some unfulfilled ambition the parent has for the child.

Parents who are so hurt and angry and may be experiencing rejection from their young adult that they decide to do the same. They cut off contact in any form with their young adult. In this approach everyone suffers—the young adult, the parent, and the relationship.

Backbone Readiness: Quiz

Are you ready to step up and take a stand? Are you ready to be supportive and loving but firm on what you will accept or not accept from your young adult? Rate your readiness to become a parent with backbone. Use the following scale and write your number in front of each statement.

0   1   2   3   4   5   6   7   8   9   10

Not at all ready   Completely ready

_____ A. I have a deep understanding of the importance of communicating my expectations and setting boundaries and sticking with them.

_____ B. I am willing to act out of love and not out of anxiety, fear, or possible rejection by my young adult.

_____ C. I believe I can be calm and manage my anxiety, fear, or hurt in the face of an angry or rejecting response from my young adult.

_____ D. I believe that I am available, accessible, and willing to listen and understand my young adult's needs and interests before I share my perspectives.

_____ E. I am willing to live with the consequences of taking a stand in the name of love and support for my young adult's progress toward mature independence.

_____ F. I am willing to change, admit when I am wrong, and be both firm and flexible. I am open to compromise and negotiation when it is in the best interest of the young adult's progress toward mature independence.

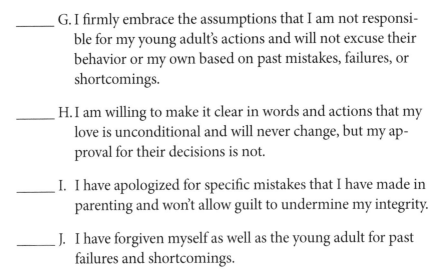

_____ G. I firmly embrace the assumptions that I am not responsible for my young adult's actions and will not excuse their behavior or my own based on past mistakes, failures, or shortcomings.

_____ H. I am willing to make it clear in words and actions that my love is unconditional and will never change, but my approval for their decisions is not.

_____ I. I have apologized for specific mistakes that I have made in parenting and won't allow guilt to undermine my integrity.

_____ J. I have forgiven myself as well as the young adult for past failures and shortcomings.

How did you score (a higher score is better)? Can you identify some actions that you need to change? Which two of your actions scored the lowest? Check them on the list. What are the actions you need to take to increase one or more of these scores? See the next section. Also consider which actions to commit to in "Call to Action" in chapter 10.

Tips to Strengthen Backbone Readiness

Review the practical tips and examples below that relate to your _lower scores_ and identify actions you could take to strengthen your backbone.

A. Deep understanding of the importance of communicating expectations and setting boundaries. The best thing to do to raise this score is to review earlier parts of this book. Take some time and write down the reasons why you need to exhibit backbone for yourself and for the sake of your young adult's progress toward mature independence. Review this list and discuss it with supportive people so you have it well embedded in your thinking.

B. Not acting out of fear or anxiety. It's really important to know that the right thing to do is to let go and let your young adult take responsibility for their life. Hard as it is to let go when you are afraid or anxious about their decisions or actions, it is what needs to happen developmentally. Understand that you don't want to be controlled by fear and anxiety and even if this does exist, you can still let go and let them be responsible. You might say as a parent, "I'm really worried about you but I know I have to back off and let go, let you make your own decisions and I will do my best to do this."

C. Staying calm and believing you can be calm is critical. We know from research that once our pulse rate gets over 100 we start to lose our ability to think rationally. Practice on staying calm, and if arguments escalate ask for a time out so you each can calm down but offer a time to come back and talk again. See managing conflict guidelines later in this book

D. Being available, accessible, and able to listen. It is important for parents to take the lead in reaching out and/or responding to their young adults in a sincere effort to understand their point of view. By doing this you earn the right to be heard and to share your perspective. This is a wired generation living in a digital world, and if we want to connect we have to participate in that world. Being present is not just connecting through different mediums; it is saying in a heartfelt way, "I am here for you."

E. Willing to live with the consequences of taking a stand. If you are acting out of love and integrity and you believe your stance toward your young adult is aimed at helping them become more independent, then you are on the right track. You need to have the higher and long-term view in mind versus being liked or accepted by your young adult in the short term. Ask yourself: Did I act out of love? Did I do what I thought was right? You may say to your angry young adult, "I'm sorry you are unhappy about my expectations and decisions, but I have to do what I think is best for you even if you end up being angry at me. I'm acting out of love and trying to support your desire to move toward more independence."

F. Willing to change, admit mistakes, and compromise. Being firm is not being rigid and never changing or compromising. Being willing to listen to your young adult, empathize, consider their point of view, and seek common ground may be a more important lesson to get across than one that says: I never change as a parent. It's helpful to acknowledge that you are new to parenting young adults as they are to being a young adult.

G. Embrace the assumption that you are not responsible for your young adult's actions. Whether your young adult's actions are in the past or present, you are not responsible, but you are responsible for your actions past and present. Both parents and young adults must acknowledge inappropriate or damaging actions in the past and not excuse them, but apologize and move on. For all of us, growing up and reaching mature independence requires letting go of the past and not using it as an excuse for current behaviors. Recognize you can't change the past—yours or theirs—but you are both responsible for your actions today.

H. My love is unconditional but my approval for words and actions by my young adult is not. My advice to parents in the workshop is to separate the messages of unconditional love from those of disapproval for certain actions. For example, if you say, "I love you, but I don't approve of . . . " the "but" part of this sentence essentially cancels out the first part of the sentence. Please separate these messages or the impact of each will be diluted at best.

I. Apologizing for mistakes made and failures as a parent. This is one of the healing parental practices that can earn you the right to be heard and appreciated. Once you apologize to the young adult you can release yourself from this guilt and are able to be firm in a loving way. For more help with this practice, go to www.parentslettinggo.com (also in the bibliography) and look for materials and the book *Apology: The Gift We Give Our Young Adults.*

J. Forgiveness. This is the other parental practice that can heal relationships between you and your young adult and create the foundation for healthy differentiation. We may try unconsciously to make up for these mistakes by giving in on requests that we know are not in the young adult's best interest. We have to demonstrate a forgiving heart both toward our young adults and ourselves if we hope to have healthy relationships. For more help with the forgiveness practice, go to www.parentslettinggo.com and check out materials and the book *Forgiveness: The Gift We Give Our Young Adults and Ourselves.*

When you believe you are stronger and ready to act with love and backbone, what approach should you take? A good starting point is to engage your young adult through an interview process aimed at better understanding them. If you have a fairly comfortable and open relationship, they may respond favorably to such an idea where they can share their perspectives. However, if you are facing a crisis, a contentious situation, or estrangement, it may be more challenging.

CHAPTER 5

Does My Young Adult Think I Have Integrity?

One of the common assignments within the six practice books is to propose an interview with the young adult to obtain their views and ideas. This is especially important when we are trying to learn what they value and hold onto as part of their identity or approach to life.

To propose an interview requires that you have established a solid relationship with your young adult and have communicated your love for them, apologized as necessary, and forgiven them and yourself for past mistakes and failures. If you don't have this solid relationship, you may need to do some work to reestablish your credibility. The interview process, when done with a sincere goal in mind of stepping back and listening for understanding, invites the young adult to move toward you. This process and sharing can support the desire of most young adults and parents to have a more friendly and satisfying relationship with each other.

> *"The interview process and questions were worth the entire workshop as it allowed me to begin a dialogue with my young adult daughter."*
> —Parent attending a Parents Letting Go workshop

The Context of the Young Adult Experience

Before engaging a young adult in the interview process, it is important to consider the context or the world of the young adult experience. Specifically, there are challenges they are facing that may influence how they may answer the interview questions. If you listen closely and well, you will hear the influences of the following factors and others in their answers.

- Young adults are trying to accomplish important developmental tasks of identity, independence, and intimacy. And I would add a desire to find purpose and happiness.

- They are a work in progress in many areas—emotionally, psychologically, and physically. In the latter case their brains are still maturing, especially the executive function that relates to logic, decision making, analytical skills, and so forth.

- They are likely experiencing some level of ambivalence about their status and future. They may feel like they are still a kid at times and at other times feel the responsibility of being an adult. They may feel ambivalent about their dependent and independent needs relative to their parents.

- They are likely to be having some anxiety about their future and maybe fears about failing in school, at work, or in relationships.

- Today's young adults are taking more time addressing their developmental tasks and are willing to experiment with and make changes in jobs, educational programs, and relationships. Note to parents: Be patient.

- They are living in a different era—the post 9/11 era of social media—with many uncertainties, economic crises, debts, and natural disasters such as Katrina.

Interview Guidelines to Help Parents Show Supportive Integrity

Do you remember when your child came home from school and told you they had an assignment to interview *you*? Maybe it was about your heritage or your job or family life. Well, turnabout is fair play. One way to establish a solid reference point for any actions you may pursue with your young adult is to start with their views. Use these guidelines.

- Begin with a sincere desire to understand them better, improve the relationship, and identify ways you can be helpful to them. Tell them this is the purpose of the interview. Think like a reporter or an anthropologist trying to understand this person and their culture.

- Listen nonjudgmentally to understand their experience and point of view and not debate these. Don't listen with a bias of what they should be experiencing or what you experienced in your young adulthood. Check for understanding if their response is unclear; it's fair to ask for examples but don't debate these or they may shut down.

- Use your best listening and reflecting skills. After each answer check for understanding or ask for clarification if needed. Refer to the book *Can You Speak Millennial "ese"?* available at www.parentslettinggo.com and brush up on your listening skills.

- Propose getting out of the house for a meal to go over the questions. Establish a more sociable and adult-to-adult venue than the home.

- Allow them to pass on any question they do not want to answer.

- If they are unwilling to meet face-to-face, offer an option of reading and recording their answers to the questions by email or text. The goal is to get the information that will help you understand them and not to control how you get this.

- Be prepared, and offer to answer any questions they may have of you with the same option to pass if you don't want to answer it. Welcome these questions as a way to foster dialogue and transparency. To not disrupt the flow of gathering their thoughts, offer to answer their questions at the end of your interview. Make a note of these and be sure to come back to them.

Tell yourself you are interviewing your young adult to listen and learn. Repeat as necessary.

The Interview Questions

Note: If you are one person interviewing a young adult, just change "we" to "I."

1. In what ways were we either too strict or too lax during your childhood?

2. What values did we try to get across to you in your younger years? What about important truths, sayings, or principles to guide you in life?

3. What one or two ideas, principles, values, or lessons would you have liked for us to teach you in your younger years?

4. In what ways do we expect too much or too little of you now?

5. If you were your own parent, what would you have done differently when you were a child? What would you do differently now if you were your own parent?

6. What are your most important values, principles, and guidelines for living your life?

7. How do you define being independent of your parents?

8. What do you think is unique about you? What sets you apart from others your age? Personality, behavior, interests?

9. As you move more toward this independence, what ways would you like to still stay connected or involved with us as your parents?

10. Where do you see yourself in five years? Where might you be living? Working? Married or with girlfriend or boyfriend?

11. How do you want us to stay in touch or communicate with you when you are on your own?

12. In what ways are we too strict or too lenient in how we approach you at this time? What suggestions do you have as to how we might strike a better balance?

13. In what ways should we step back, let go, and allow you to make your own decisions?

14. In what ways do you want us to be more supportive or helpful to you?

15. What do you think is your purpose in life, or what you would most like to accomplish or experience?

16. What is the source of happiness in your life?

The questions focus on certain themes: independence, identity, purpose, feedback to parents how to be helpful, and so forth. Once this information is gathered, you may have a better idea of how you want to approach your young adult. There is nothing sacred about this list, and you should feel free to make up your own questions. There are two caveats if you wish to generate your own questions.

First, be sure that the questions will be useful in understanding your young adult and how you can more effectively relate to them. Second, don't use this as a secret way to try to get at concerns that you might have. For example, if you have a concern about your young adult being sexually active, don't ask for their view on premarital sex to try to find this out. Keep this off this list and interview process. Instead, be straightforward in your request and do it at a different time. After taking the time to learn about and understand your young adult and show a sincere interest in responding to their needs, it's time to clarify the process of exhibiting backbone.

CHAPTER 6

How Do I Show My Young Adult I Have Integrity?

Although each situation or challenge parents face is unique and personal, there are some general guidelines that can be applied. The following key guidelines and examples can help parents show integrity and make the best decisions in helping their young adults transition to mature independence.

Be clear about your values and principles and be willing to share these with your young adult. Make a list of what you believe are the important values to which you ascribe. Google the words *values*, *integrity*, and *character* and reflect on what you believe are values you want to embrace. Make another list of factors you believe are important in family relationships and in society at large. You may ask your young adult to do the same and then compare your lists. My guess is your responses will not be too far apart. Truth, transparency, respect, honesty, caring, loyalty, responsibility, independence, and cooperation are a few that come to mind.

Don't measure the success of your advice to your young adult based solely on their response and actions. This is particularly true in the short term. Many adolescents and young adults are trying to establish their independence in thought and action and may resist your guidance. Whether this is the case or not, remember the basic assumption that we can't control our young adults. If they don't want to do something, we may not be able to force them to do it. This includes those living at home. However, if they are living at home you have leverage because they are receiving certain benefits, such as shelter, food, and so forth. As such their stay at home may be contingent on following your advice. But ultimately they have the choice and power to say no and leave.

So how do we evaluate our efforts? Look in the mirror and do your own report card. Ask yourself: Was I loving? Was I true to my values? Did I do what I think was right to help my young adult move toward mature independence? This relates to taking responsibility for your actions refer-  enced in laying the foundation in chapter 1. Consider the long-term value of taking a stand versus the short-term reaction, and realize that they will benefit from your actions, if not acknowledge the value of them, at a later time.

Adopt a different parenting style to accommodate the developmental needs of young adults. As children age, they need to be given more freedom and more responsibility, which requires the parent to move back from a more directive or authoritarian role. In *Can You Speak Millennial "ese"?* these different parenting roles are described in more depth. Parents need to move from provider and protector to partner with their young adult. In this regard, new skills need to be learned and adopted. There may still be a place for being directive and implementing certain rules and consequences if the young adult is at home, however the natural developmental process would argue for less of this. It is important to engage your young adult *as* a young adult with the freedom and responsibility they have to make their own decisions, and indicate that you would like to provide some input.

The three ways you can provide this input is to use the three Cs: coaching, consulting, and collaborating.

- *Coaching* is being available to ask questions and help them explore new options and ideas—pros and cons of their decisions but not offering your ideas or advise. Your role is to help  them to think and come up with their own solutions.

- *Consulting* is like being a business consultant. You can offer them ideas, suggestions, resources, and your learnings but being careful to qualify this input as something they can consider and reject. Consultants in companies give their best advice but the decisions always remain with the company. I reiterate this routinely with my young adult children after I share an opinion. On one occasion I hesitated to give my advice to my son on an internship he was considering. He said, "Dad, just tell me what you would do. I will still make my own decision." So I did and he made his own decision, which happened to match mine. I think he felt like he got my advice and was able to make a decision that was his but aligned with my advice without giving up his freedom to choose other options.

- *Collaborating* is standing side by side with your young adult to find ways to work together, areas to compromise, and win-wins. Avoid fostering a situation that suggests it is a parent's way or one where the young adult feels a need to demonstrate independence and choose a different path just to show independence.

Risk the discomfort and have the courage to ask the tough questions. Following is an example from my private practice that relates to this topic.

The mother of a twenty-three-year-old young adult I was seeing in my private practice confided in me that she thought her daughter was suffering from gender dysphoria: the condition of feeling one's emotional and psychological identity as male or female to be opposite to one's biological sex. She had been worried about this since high school because of some comment her daughter had made. Recently, observing her daughter's commitment to fitness and becoming a personal trainer only added to this concern. She finally approached her daughter who told her mother not to be concerned that "she liked boys." The point is not to suggest a judgmental approach to someone who may have gender dysphoria, but that the mother had worried needlessly because she was unwilling to broach the subject with her daughter.

Our time with our young adults is short. Don't waste this time sitting on some concern or fear that you have that holds you back from approaching your young adult honestly. These undisclosed questions or concerns will undermine your relationship with them. Approach your young adult with honesty and a willingness to acknowledge that you are having difficulty raising a concern but need to be honest with them.

Pick your battles and be willing to seek common ground, compromises, and solutions. A hot button for parents is when their authority or expertise is challenged, and they know or believe they are right. Some of this comes from old school training when we were growing up and we heard the explanation for why we should do something: BECAUSE I SAID SO. Even though we hated that phrase from our parents, we often absorbed that voice of our parents and find such statements spewing forth from our mouths. Sometimes we are shocked to hear what sounds like our mother or father's voice coming out of our mouth. Some of us have a harder time giving up authority and being right, and this can create a problem in our relationship with our young adults.

When making a decision, first determine who and how the decision is to be made. Is it totally up to the young adult or do you need to come to some mutually agreed upon outcome? If it is totally up to the young adult, use consulting and coaching skills but they make the decision and are fully responsible for the consequences of the decision. On the other hand if parents are paying for college, they may want some say in the selection of schools and the costs associated with this, and the final decision may need to be mutual. A good bit of confusion and conflict can be avoided by first deciding how and who will make the final decision.

Work with your young adult to come up with guidelines for handling conflict. If you are fighting constantly, maybe you're stuck in trying to control everything and may need to just let some things go. Here are some suggested guidelines for when you face conflict; stick with them even if your young adult is violating them.

- No violence or threats of violence.

- No swearing or personal attacks.

- Listen without interrupting and state what you heard the other person say and allow clarification before communicating your position.

- Avoid starting with "you." Start with "I" and express your feelings, observations, and perceptions. Don't say, "I think you are lazy." That's a dirty "I" statement. Say, "I am upset and concerned that you are watching TV when you could be out looking for a job."

- Make every effort to stay calm and not get hooked into violating these guidelines. Slow down your breathing and keep your voice calm even if your young adult raises their voice.

- If you are stuck in an argument with no resolution or the tone is escalating and you feel uncomfortable, ask for a time out, but whoever calls time out must state a time back in before ending the discussion. This should be within twenty-four hours at the outer limit. Too many people in conflict just walk away and issues never get addressed. Calling a time out indicates that you believe that the argument is escalating, becoming destructive, or de-railing, and you want to stop this pattern. Stating a time back in indicates that you value the relationship, think the issue is important, and want to come back to it when you both have calmed down. Use the time to brainstorm solutions you could propose that would satisfy both parties when you time back in.

- Seek repair after a difficult argument where one or the other may have violated the rules or said something they regret. Offer an apology for any part you played relative to the issue or how you argued about it. You don't have to take all of the responsibility—"It takes two to tango." Warning: Don't apologize and then say "but, however" and then point out a failure on the young adult's part or you will just reignite the argument.

My personal experience with this last point on dealing with arguments indicates how difficult this is. I grew up very defensive and could always find someone or something to blame. At one point my parents thought I should be a lawyer because I was so good at arguing, deflecting, and projecting blame. It was very hard to begin to apply this apology for some part of the conflict with my wife without following it with "but you . . ." After a good bit of practice both of us have been able to repair after a destructive argument by taking some responsibility for some part we played in this without blaming the other.

Note: For more on how to be effective in apologizing to your young adult see *Apology: The Gift We Give Our Young Adults* on the website parentslettinggo.com. On the concept of "repairing" see the work of John Gottman and Nan Silver in the bibliography on p. 79.

No is not a four-letter word. No is not a bad word and is necessary to letting go and letting the young adult grow to mature indepen-dence. It takes backbone to say no, but it can be the most caring and empowering word you can say to your young adult.

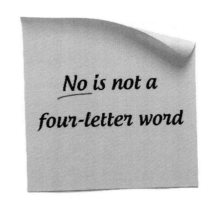

- No does not mean you don't care.

- No can be very empowering. Forcing the young adult to do something of which you know they are capable can result in increased confidence.

- No does not mean you are rejecting them but may be a request you cannot support.

- No allows the young adult to face the consequences of their ac-tions and is a chance to learn from failure or mistakes.

- No helps build resilience and self-efficacy.

- No can mean that you are not going to intervene and fix some-thing they have done.

- No means that you won't cover for, excuse, or rationalize your young adult's behavior.

- No means being true to your values in word and actions.

While in college my youngest daughter called me one night sobbing about how her roommates had ditched her and went out to eat. She felt terribly rejected and asked me to come and pick her up. There is some-thing for having your young adult attend college in another state as opposed to five miles away. What I said to her was that I wouldn't come and get her, that she had great interpersonal skills, and I was sure she

37

could work this out with her roommates. She said, "So you are not coming to pick me up?" My response, "Correct." The next night she called and I asked how things were going with her roommates. "Oh fine" she said, "I talked to them and we're good."

When considering saying no, ask yourself three questions. If the answer is yes to each one, then stand firm.

- Is this the loving action to take as a parent?

- Is this the right action to take in terms of my principles and values?

- Will this ultimately help my young adult move toward mature independence?

When did you take a stand with your young adult now or in the past, although unpopular, that turned out to be the right decision?

Have and use a strong support network. A network could include spouse, friends, family members, or professionals who will support you in demonstrating backbone with your young adult. There's a saying by Augusten Burroughs:
"Your mind is like an unsafe neighborhood; don't go there alone." Good advice for all of us parents. We need other parents and supportive people in our lives to keep us grounded and able to stand up for our values and beliefs with our young adults. It's great to have a partner to discuss the ways to approach your young adult and how to apply the principles in this book. If you are a single parent, find some other parents or friends with whom you can obtain feedback on your thinking and plans of handling your young adult.

**Use a goal-setting process aimed at meeting both the parents'
and the young adult's goals over a set period of time.** A good
starting point is with the goals of the young adult five years in the
future. Ask the young adult to come up with them. Simultaneously
the parents should come up with their desired goals for the young
adult in the same five-year block of time. Discuss the extent to which
the goals by both parties match up. Come to an agreement on these
goals. In most cases young adults come up with fairly traditional
goals: job, apartment, car, significant other, and so forth, which the
parents can readily support. I've never had a young adult indicate
that their five-year goal was to become a pothead and sleep on the
beach.

Parents should ask how they could support the goals of the young
adult over the next five years. From this point, the young adult
should identify interim actions or accomplishments over the next
three years, one year, six months, and one month that will help them
make progress toward the five-year plan. The parents should commit
to certain actions that they will take over the same time period to
support their young adult's goals. Establish a time every two weeks to
review progress on goals and don't nag or question the young adult
between these meetings. Over time you may wish to extend these
update meetings to monthly.

Manage the dance. Do your best to
manage the dance between you and your
young adult. Try to be sensitive to when
they are pulling away in a healthy manner and reinforce or praise this; but also
recognize when they are moving toward
you for reassurance, advice, affirmation,
or maybe just a hug. The path to mature
independence is a zigzag line with various
side trips and bumps along the way.

> *"But I try to back off and when I do, they mess up or do something irresponsible and I get sucked back in."*
>
> —A parent comment

In my clinical practice, I am often seeing parents of late adolescents or young adults who unfortunately are acting in ways that force the parents back into a disciplinary role. When these setbacks occur, it is important to take a measured approach that continues to deliver consequences but acknowledges the need of the young adult to move forward in their development. What do I mean by this? If they are living at home, driving a family car, and received a speeding ticket, rather than a total ban on the use of the car, which represents independence and capability of pursuing their interests, consider limited use such as getting to school or work. Or the young adult may be restricted from using the car on odd days for two weeks with a review after a week, and if there are no problems, the use of the car can be increased. Without the use of the car, there may be no way to demonstrate reforming their behavior in a way that warrants further use of the car.

CHAPTER 7

How Do I Handle My Challenging Situation?

Young Adult Living at Home or Bouncing Back and Forth

"I'm Back!"

It's important to understand and accept that in American culture, moving out and on is a natural development stage in the family life cycle. Both parents and young adults are wired up to let go and separate. There has never been a time when I have asked a young adult over the age of eighteen where he or she wanted to live five years from now that they answered, "I just want to be living with mom and dad." It just doesn't happen. At the same time living at home does not necessarily constitute a failure of this stage of development.

Moving out should not be the primary focus but rather supporting the young adult's actions that move toward mature independence.

I am not in the camp that says there is a specific date the young adult needs to be out of the home. That's not to say you may not have to force the issue in some cases. There are clearly young adults living at home who have achieved mature independence, and there are young adults living outside the home who have not. There is also a risk that a primary if not exclusive focus on when the young adult will be moving out can create a sense of insecurity and rejection and trigger resistance. Another factor that has delayed the moving out and on is that many parents (over 60 percent) enjoy having their adult children living at home.[3]

Following are some typical reasons young adults move out. They apply to the both those living at home and those who have bounced back to the comfort of the homeland.

1. They want to move out whether they believe they can do this successfully or not. It's not uncommon for a young adult to find a girlfriend or boyfriend for whom living with the parents and their house rules doesn't go over well. They need to have the chance to make it on their own.

2. The parents want to have more time to themselves and to be able to come and go, travel, or otherwise spend time together, post empty nest, without having to feel responsible for another person living at the house. It's okay to desire this. You also may be facing retirement and reduced income to support three or more adults. There's a lot to say for the empty nest stage. More on the "empty nest" experience in Book Six - *Growing Apart: Letting Go of Our Young Adults.*

3. The parents want to move to a vacation place or downsize their current house and there will not be room for the young adult. (I don't think I have ever heard of parents who decided to travel the country in an RV taking their young adult with them.)

4. When you see a young adult comfortable at home and not pursuing responsible mature independent behavior, it may be time to institute an exit plan. There is a term the Japanese use to describe the situation of a young adult languishing at home: *hikikomori* means "being too content" or " too comfortable."

5. When living together leads to many conflicts and arguments about rules, expectations, and responsibilities around the house, it's time for a change. For example, a young adult living at home

brings illicit drugs in and vapes with electronic cigarettes after his mother pleaded with him to stop because the smell bothered her. Is he ready to go relative to demonstrating mature independence? No! But he is ready to live somewhere else because he is not willing to go along with the house rules? Yes! His actions are saying he wants to live somewhere else. You are not kicking him out, you are honoring his wishes.

6. When there are threats made or violence by either parents or young adults, it is time to part ways. If as a parent you are living in such a threatening situation, you may need to call the police and have the young adult removed. You don't have a responsibility to an eighteen-year-old to house that young adult and under such circumstances, for your sake as well as the young adult's, you have to have them removed.

If the decision is made for them to be living at home for the immediate future, the expectation is that they work on being an independent and responsible adult living with the parents. When working with families of young adults living at home, I ask them to try to view the young adult as a boarder or roommate. This is most likely the status the young adult will transition to in leaving. It is unlikely that the young adult would move directly to a home and live alone. More likely the young adult would move in with a roommate, friend, or boyfriend or girlfriend. A lack of privacy for time with a partner or pressure from that partner to stop living with mom and dad is often the key impetus for their moving on. So the more you can create the experience they will likely have when they move out the easier it will be for them to make the transition. Also, identify the basic milestones that the young adult needs to achieve to become a mature, independent adult and begin to coach and consult with the young adult, as invited, on attaining these.

Actions to foster a healthy relationship with your young adult at home

While you and the young adult are sharing your home, there are ways to foster a healthy relationship.

1. Take some time outside of the home, possibly for breakfast, to discuss where the young adult wishes to be in five years. Ask them to write these out. Where will they be living? Here or another state? How much will they be paying for rent or a mortgage? Will they be living alone or with a roommate? Girlfriend or boyfriend? Will they have a job? What type of job? What do they think they will be making a year in the job? Will they have a car? What type of car? How will they be spending their free time? Will they be coming over for dinner if they are in town? How do they envision the relationship with you five years from now once they are on their own? The interview questions described earlier (page 28) can serve as a good starting point and then move into the transition questions at a subsequent meeting.

2. Discuss with them the concept of becoming more of an adult and roommate in the home and identifying a time that they believe would be good to move out. Explain that the approach is one where you want them to participate as a roommate because they will likely face this when they move out. If they have been to college and lived in a dorm or house with other students, they should be able to identify with this type of living arrangement. It may be a little easier if they lived in a house or apartment and had to prepare meals versus a dorm room and eating in a cafeteria. In either case, remind them that they have already experienced the roommate role and should be able to master this.

3. Explain how the relationship will need to change with the new adult roommate arrangement. What does the young adult expect in changes from the parents with the new role. How do they think the parent should change in treating them like a roommate? What do the parents expect from the young adult in this new role?

4. Identify and practice changes that the parents should make so as to not treat the young adult as if they were fifteen: Did you eat dinner? What time did you get up? Come home? It is more diffi-

cult to change than you might believe because parents and young adults regress into old parent-child patterns naturally or unconsciously. For example, Parent: "Are you playing video games all day long? How are you going to be successful sitting around playing games?" Young adult: "Why are you always nagging me about playing video games? I play with my friends. What's the big deal?"

Expectation guidelines

It is important to consider guidelines for expectations related to a young adult living at home. Following are some to suggestions (also some cautions).

1. Go to school or have a job, any job, but have income. The young adult may still be waiting for the perfect job that fits their degree or major, but in the meantime, the young adult is expected to work.

2. Pay rent. The young adult should be expected to pay some amount toward rent because that would be what the young adult would experience on their own. You can make an exception to this if the young adult is attending school or you can cover some costs of school and expect them to work part time and provide a minimal amount of rent. I advise parents to put the rent money into an account that you can give to the young adult when they move out to pay for a security deposit and first month's rent.

3. Establish a living space for them where they can come and go comfortably. It could be a basement area or someplace where they can watch a TV or play video games, but not in the common area.

4. Outline specific ways the young adult will need to take care of their own areas of responsibility: clean their room, do their

laundry, buy essential items like toiletries, and pay their cell phone bill, gas for the car, auto insurance, and so forth. No longer having cell phone service paid for may stimulate the need for employment. The more they can take responsibility for being independent and responsible for their lifestyle choices the easier the transition to living on their own.

5. Establish guidelines for common areas: Don't leave clothes, food, or other items in the common areas. Identify certain responsibilities of the household and indicate that the young adult has to take on X number per week. These can be things like cleaning the house, making meals, outside work, and shop for and contribute food. Give some choice of chores but retain the right to set the number of chores. Ones they don't take fall on the parents.

6. Other guidelines may include when they come in at night, and the need to be quiet since the parents likely need to get up for work in the morning. This goes for staying up late at night as well as being considerate and quiet. There may need to be some guidelines of having friends over and if parents need to be home or not. If requests are made for money, set up guidelines for when and how and how much you should help them. In the end, don't do anything for them that they can do themselves, and if they need help on something, they need to step up and do their part first.

7. Set up a check-in time every two weeks to discuss what is working and what isn't; problem solve together. It may be best to go out to breakfast and discuss how the arrangements are working since it feels more adult-to-adult than in the home. In the meantime don't nag but keep track of things that are being done by the young adult and things that are not being done per the family guidelines. When meeting, start with what's going right and working.

8. Offer consultation on money management, budgeting, finding jobs, finding places to live, car maintenance, and so forth. It is surprising how many young adults today have never changed a

tire. None of my three young adults have. Change the oil? Don't know if they could find the dipstick! These types of services are readily available so our young people have not found a need to learn these things, but they should know how to get help with things like these even if they don't do them. Be willing to ask for their help as well as offer yours as that equalizes the relationship. My son has set up most of the electronics in my house.

Some cautions

- I am not of the school that parents should find ways to make it very uncomfortable for young adults to live at home, such as give them a cot in a bare room, limit their use of other parts of the house, or tell them they can't eat the food in the refrigerator. At the same time, it's important to give them space and support any responsible independent action they take. My assumption and evidence I have accumulated indicate that they want to eventually be on their own so my approach is to capitalize on this drive.

- Manipulative efforts are not appropriate, such as saying you will buy them furniture or help them buy a car if they leave. These kinds of bribes can backfire and you might find not only your young adult back home but you now have a car loan and a bunch of furniture.

- Some parents write up very "legalistic" contracts. You can google contracts with adolescents or young adults to see some templates. Not sure that this is the best approach, although some parents have had success with this. I prefer the more organic process of sitting down with a pad of paper, writing out the guidelines, and having both the parent and young adult sign it with the idea you will review it at the two week check-in meeting and revise as necessary. It's good to have it in writing but don't think that doing so is the magic. Following the agreements is much more about the spirit than the law. It has more likelihood of success through mutual understanding and respect for the process of letting go and supporting mature independence than nailing down every possible rule and potential infractions. I would also choose "agreement" over "contract" for the language. My desire is to not create unnecessary resistance, and many times the legalistic approach triggers anger and resistance right from the beginning. That said, here are a couple of websites that describe living at home contracts: http://adultchildrenlivingathome.com and http://www.contract-template.org/parentchild-contract-for-an-adult-child-living-at-home.html.

Areas to cover in an agreement

Following are some things that should be in a living at home agreement.

Purpose of the agreement: To outline expectations of the living arrangements and responsibilities of both parents and (*young adult's name*) that will ensure we can have a positive experience in living together. This arrangement is temporary to provide an opportunity to transition to the young adult's own living arrangements outside of the home. The expectations and responsibilities as outlined below will be reviewed every two weeks by parents and (*young adult's name*) at which times adjustments in the terms can be considered.

Expectations: some to consider for the young adult.

- Rent-specific expectations: amount, due date, and so forth (parents may retain rent and make available when young adult leaves).

- Purchasing/chipping in on food, cooking (x nights week), laundry, and chores.

- Attendance at school and/or job.

- Quiet hours: everybody needs to sleep especially parents if working and need to get up in the morning.

- Use of car, gas, upkeep.

- Insurance on vehicle.

- Cell phone.

- Guests and any overnight restrictions.

- Specific prohibitions if needed: no alcohol use if minor, no illegal drugs in house or being used.

- No violence or threats of violence or damage to property.

- Respect by all members of the household: no swearing, name-calling, or personal attacks.

Expectations: some to consider for the parent.

- Show the investment the parents are making (optional).

- Provide a bedroom, bed, access to other areas of house, TV, computer.

- Provide x meals a week and x amount of food for young adult to eat at other times.

- Will maintain the house: clean common areas, provide sheets and bedding.

- Will respect young adult's privacy and desire to be independent.

- Will provide consultation and coaching as requested by young adult.

- Will cover all costs related to house: mortgage, insurance, utilities, Cable or other TV access, and Wi-Fi.

This agreement will be reviewed every two weeks and adjusted as agreed upon by all parties. If (*young adult's name*) does not adhere to the requirements of this agreement, a period of thirty days probation will be established. If (*young adult's name*) does not comply within this thirty-day period, (*young adult's name*) will be asked to find alternative living arrangements within the next thirty days.

Date of agreement: _____

Parties to the agreement: _____   _____

_____

If a young adult fails to comply with the agreement, an alternative to having them move out immediately is to offer some consequences for such noncompliance. If they indicate a desire to stay and a willingness to recommit to the expectations, then one short-term option is to require them to do some extra community service around the house or pay a fine. It could be some project you haven't gotten to like cleaning the garage. Or possibly tap into some skill/interest they have such as pulling information together for you from the Internet—maybe to find a plan about how to transition out of the home if they are not comfortable complying with the house rules and expectations!

Your ultimate leverage is to help them pack and move out. It shouldn't be seen as necessarily a bad outcome or failure if they don't seem to be willing to comply with living at home expectations; so don't think of kicking them out in a punishing way. Rather, explain to them that they must need to be on their own where they can live the way they want to and make their own decisions, and you will provide some help to them to move out. On this last point, if you have saved some money from rent they paid that could be used as a deposit on an apartment, but they need to do the work to find a roommate and a place to live.

When working with families of adolescents, I like to put expectations into three categories. First, deal breakers. These are actions that would preclude them living at home and plans are made immediately for their exit. If under age this may be to a group home. These are actions they might take such as destroying things in the house, threatening or using physical violence, using drugs and/or bringing them into the house, or stealing from the parents. This category shouldn't be more than about five clear rules that lead to the decision that they can no longer live at home.

Second are expectations for which you have consequences and renegotiate periodically: chores, clean room, do laundry, cook one or two meals, and so forth. This applies to adolescents but if you have young adult-post high school or college kids, you hope that they would see the expectations above as those that reflect adult shared responsibilities.

Third, discretionary behaviors (their decision): dress, music, video games, tattoos/piercing, friends, social activities, travel, and food choices.

At the end of the day, it's your house. You set the rules and expectations, which should be reasonable, but your young adult needs to meet these or if they don't want to or by their actions indicate that they don't agree with the rules and expectations, they are choosing to leave.

Young Adult Living outside the Home without Significant Health Concerns

Free at last they are out of the house!

Not so fast. Clearly there are some benefits when a young adult is living outside the home. No more daily skirmishes over house rules and guidelines. They live in an apartment with friends and come and go as they please. There is a comfort in the old adage: Out of sight out of mind.

My wife and I experienced the challenge of having college students return for vacations in the summer, and we experienced a return of a sense of responsibility for where they were, what they were doing, when they would be home, when they would get up, and so forth. It's 1:00 in the morning, and they're downstairs cooking up something to eat, pots rattling, and the noise of the TV. Or worse it's two and they are not home. Where are they? Did they have an accident? Should we call and see if they are okay? Once they moved out for good we slept better. Ignorance is bliss.

Overall, for empty nesters the benefits to the couple and their stage in the family life cycle outweigh the costs, particularly if you can maintain an amiable relationship and regular communication with your young adult.

Guidelines and actions

What are the guidelines that should apply in this situation? This situation highlights the key assumption that you cannot control your young adult. In fact you don't even know what they are doing or not doing, particularly if they are discrete and resistant to discussing their personal lives. When they were living at home you had leverage, a "say so," because they were trading their freedom for the benefits of a roof over their heads, food, safety, and other comforts. You could also observe them and even communicate with them at times. Now you don't have that same type of leverage—meaning the power to influence a person or a situation. In some cases, young adults move out but the parents still fund a lot of their expenses, such as the cost of an apartment, school, insurances, car, and so forth. If you are doing all of these things, then you do have leverage, but it may be difficult to back away from such action.

1. Start with an understanding of your young adult's goals and aspirations. If you have not done the exercise about interviewing your young adult (page 28) this would be a good time to do that. Begin a conversation with, "Now that you are living on your own, I'd like to hear more about your plans and interests, but I want you

to know I can no longer tell you what you can and can't do. I will just listen unless you want some input or feedback from me." You can ask them about their five-year plan. Where do they want to be living five years from now? What will they be doing? What job or school will they be involved with? Will they be married or in a serious relationship?

2. Another discussion is one about how you would like the new relationship between you and them to be. Ask them how you can stay in touch and be of some support or help to you as they venture forth on their own. It's also a time to clarify any support that they would like to have from you and what kinds of things you are willing to do and not do. Sometimes parents are the problem and want to continue to stay involved and take care of the young adult. When we took our daughter to college we talked with the dean who decried the tendency of today's parents to be overinvolved in their kids lives. The term *helicopter parents* is often used to describe this. For example, parents go with their young adult to register for classes, contact their professors if they don't like the grade their young adult received, and more. One parent at my daughter's college came in from out of town every day to make her son's bed, clean his room and take his laundry to be washed. This helicopter parent had landed.

3. If you are in a two-parent home, be clear as a couple what funding you will make available, if any, and for what reasons. Discuss how the funding will help them with their goals and their path to mature independence. Parents need to agree on any funding before they meet with the young adult. It's appropriate to elicit information about their needs and desires, but don't negotiate with your partner in front of them. Present a united front. In general, parents should not give a blank check but consider funding some part of the young adult's expenses. Now I can hear some parents who are reading this saying, "No way, I didn't get any help with school or my expenses so why should I do that for my young adult." You have to make that decision. I would say times have

changed and there are more expenses and expensive schools than in my day along with less economic opportunity. I don't believe there is a right or wrong on this.

4. Don't do for them what they can do for themselves or at a minimum meet them half way. Offer "matching grants." Take on or subsidize some critical costs such as car or health insurance. Offer decreasing financial support to help them get on their feet. For instance, you may use a decreasing contribution to help them get into an apartment. Be creative to ensure that they have a financial stake in what you are offering.

5. Don't compromise your values or principles in terms of how they treat you or their relationship to the house. Disrespect (swearing at you) is not acceptable and there are rules regarding reentering the house and what they can haul out. They need to learn to ask permission to take stuff and call ahead if they are dropping by.

6. Make every effort to treat them in a more adult fashion. Have them over for dinner, go out to eat, let them pay the bill, split it, or have them cover the tip. Praise and reinforce all of their actions that are consistent with moving toward greater independence and responsibility. Be graceful and forgiving when they screw up, as they will, and remember your own miscues at this stage of life.

7. Discuss or follow their lead relative to frequency and form of communication. Most young adults prefer to text these days but if they prefer phone calls or emails that's fine as well. There is much more communication between parents and young adults now than in any past generation.

8. In some cases, young adults have moved out of the home and have cut off communication with the parents. These parents may or may not know why this cutoff has occurred. Sometimes the cutoff is related to your young adult partner's needs or influence. Whatever the reason, it is by far one of the most frustrating and helpless situations you can face. If you are facing this, I recommend reading Joshua Coleman's book entitled *When Parents Hurt: Compassionate*

Strategies When You and Your Grown Child Don't Get Along (see the bibliography on page 79) or visit www.drjoshuacoleman.com. This is an area Coleman addresses in depth. Rejection and being cut off from communication is only one of the many complicating factors parents face in launching young adults. The next three sections discuss some others.

The Young Adult with Mental Health or Chemical Dependency Problems

The receptive young adult with mental health or chemical dependency problems presents an opportunity for the parent to partner with them to find the help that they need. This receptivity is a welcome opportunity that sadly doesn't happen that often. Many older adolescents and young adults resist acknowledging that they have one or the other of these problems due to shame, denial, or a need or belief they can handle it on their own. Here are some steps that can be taken with a young adult with special needs who is receptive.

1. Review the assumptions at the outset of this book (page 3) and determine to approach the young adult with these in mind.

2. Assume an underlying desire for independence even though the young adult may be fearful of this.

3. Reassure the young adult that no matter what, your love for them is unconditional and you will stand with them in getting help.

4. Address any needs you may believe exist or have been expressed by the young adult for actions of apology and forgiveness. If you feel guilt or some sense of responsibility for the special need the young adult has, it may be important for you to deepen your understanding and application of these two healing practices.

Refresh your understanding of when and how to take action on the practices of apology and forgiveness by referring to the website parentslettinggo.com. See tips on these and the expression of unconditional love posted on the website or consider ordering one or more of the books on these topics.

5. If you sense they are depressed or suffering from other mental health problems, make it a condition of living at home that they seek help and offer to pay for this if you have insurance or maybe split the bill if there is not insurance. Reach out to the young adult and express your concern and desire to support their help-seeking behavior. Work with them to find the right providers and treatment professionals if they request your help. On the other hand, if they want to totally take on this task of finding the right resource, give them that latitude. The more they can do on their own the better.

6. If they are living at home, treat them as capable of meeting responsibilities such as those outlined in an agreement (pages 48–50). Again, expect more than you would normally expect of them. This sends a message that they are capable and responsible. You might be surprised as to how much they can step up when parents expect this and believe in them and their ability. You have to be realistic, but my experience is that parents often expect too little, do too much, and don't provide enough "stretch." But there is no black-and-white answer for this, and parents have to trust their heads, hearts, and the support of various services and professionals to calibrate the right level of demand.

7. If you question their ability to live on their own, you may want to seek professional advice. You may set up family counseling, or if your young adult is unwilling to go, you may need to seek help yourself in coping with the situation. A good resource for parents who are suffering with an adolescent/young adult with mental health issues is *When Your Adult Child Breaks Your Heart: Coping with Mental Illness, Substance Abuse, and the Problems That Tear Families Apart* by Joel L. Young and Christine Adamec.

The Special Needs Young Adult with Significant Mental or Physical Disabilities

All of the assumptions outlined at the start of this book apply, in most instances, with special needs populations. The exception is that they may not be capable of being responsible for all of their actions, and you may need to take some responsibility for them. If you have a young adult who is disabled physically or mentally or dealing with learning problems such as ADHD or Autism Spectrum Disorder (ASD) such as Asperger Syndrome, you may be facing some very difficult decisions about living at home or outside the home, special services needed, and so forth. I have two colleagues who had to make the painful decision to move their autistic adolescents into a group or special home because they could no longer provide the twenty-four hour coverage that these boys needed. Both of these boys have adapted, are well cared for in group homes, and are visited by the parents or brought home on weekends to be with the family. Although I have not had to deal with this difficult challenge myself, my belief is that these young adults with special needs should be given opportunities to pursue as much independence and choice as possible, experience community, and live in an environment that is best equipped to deal with their 24-7 needs.

A good research-based resource is a publication by the Agency for Healthcare Research and Quality entitled "Interventions for Adolescents and Young Adults with Autism Spectrum Disorders" available at www.ahrq.gov. Another similar government resource is available through the National Institute of Mental Health entitled "Autism Spectrum Disorders—Learn the Signs and Ask for Help if You Are Concerned" available at https://www.nimh.nih.gov/health/publications/autism-spectrum-disorder/index.shtml.

In these cases of physical or mental disability, parents are well advised to seek professional advice. Although there are no clear rules, there are guidelines that can aid you in deciding on the proper level of care, and there are professionals who can provide this guidance. This special needs area is beyond the scope of this book. If this is your situation, do some Internet research on help for young adults with certain conditions. Work with the schools, county services, and national associations to find an appropriate treatment strategy and plan.

Parents of Young Adults Who Are Married or Partnered (with or without Children)

Another challenge that parents face is that of working out their relationships with daughters-in-law and sons-on-law, and in some cases grandchildren. I was surprised when a group of these parents showed up at my workshops. These are parents who are worried about their grandchildren or find themselves caring for the grand-children sometimes as an "entitled" expectation of their young adult son or daughter. This childcare by grandparents has increased in the last ten to fifteen years as dual-career, married young adults have struggled to pay for childcare, work full time, and pay off school loans. On the other hand, some of these grandparents have com-plained about their young adult being very restrictive in allowing access to grandchildren. Beyond childcare, quite a few young adult couples still depend on their parents for financial support. This undermines the ability and sense that the young adults have of being truly independent and causes the parents to wonder how and when how they will get these young adults off the payroll.

One parent I am counseling is providing help to her forty-five-year-old son who is divorced with children. She is providing a house for him to live in for which he makes payments most of the time. But he has struggled in business, and she has had to continue to bail him out when bills mount up. It's a stretch to call these situations "failures to launch" but it likely feels a bit this way for both parties. Failing to launch is not confined to a specific age group. This group of parents and the unique challenges they face deserve their own book but is beyond the scope of this book.

In all the situations described above, there is the challenge of the parent's desire and ability to influence their young adult's decisions and actions. Often the young adult is resistant to the parent's effort to control, direct, fix, or otherwise get the young adult to do what the parent wants. Although the parent cannot control the young adult, there are some actions that parents can take to influence. The books in this series describe practices that are foundational to support the launching of young adults. If these practices—understanding, unconditional love, apology, forgiveness, integrity, and letting go—are not addressed, specific influencing techniques will be less effective and could potentially further alienate the young adult from the parent. We can't skip over these practices and think that there is some "silver bullet" technique to use to influence young adults in a direction we think they need to go. Keep in mind the goal is to influence them in the direction of the appropriate developmental tasks of identity, independence, and intimacy so that they achieve mature adulthood.

CHAPTER 8

I Can't Control My Young Adult but Can I Influence Them?

The starting point related to influence is to remember the assumption that we cannot control our young adults. At best we may be able to influence them, but they hold the power and can say no, walk away, or take other actions of

which we don't approve. We are best served to have a goal of influence, but not of expectations. Here's the distinction. A goal is to do the kinds of things that might influence a young adult. An expectation is to believe, if not assume, that your actions will produce certain changes or results. With a goal, we can measure our success by taking the right and loving action. With an expectation, we set ourselves up for disappointment if the young adult doesn't respond favorably to our influence. We also need to practice the assumption that our young adults are responsible for their lives and actions. What we can do is to continue to love them, tell them they matter to us, and let them know we are available to support them emotionally. Following are some approaches to influencing our young adults.

A Default Approach

My guess is that we all use this approach to some extent, particularly if we are not consciously trying to use a different approach. This is the default approach to influencing our young adults and managing the resistance to change we may experience with them. You may recognize this as the voice that comes out of you that sounds uncomfortably like that of your mother or father. We were raised a certain way with certain values, words, and modeling that we have put into our autopilot or long-term memory. When things get tense, we are likely to revert back to long-term, autopilot memory. If our parents did a good job, that might not be so bad. However, we are living in a different time and have likely raised our children differently so that the past generation's approach to parenting of young adults might not fit now.

When I work with couples, I focus on helping them build a conscious marriage driven by clear values and thoughts, not one run by subconscious learnings from the past. Likewise, in working with parents, it's important for them to process what they may have learned through the filters of love, support for independence, and their values. This book surfaces principles, qualities, and approaches that you might consider as an alternative to "the way my parents dealt with me in my twenties." I'm not advocating to ignore what you learned from your parents but rather stepping back and asking yourself: Is this the best approach with what I have learned through my experience and through reading this book?

Tough Love

There is a school of thought that supports a "tough love" approach by parents to their adolescents and young adults. What does this mean and how did this way of thinking start? As best I can tell, the idea of tough love comes from a book written by a colleague of mine when I was doing youth work in an organization called Young Life. The book is *Tough Love* and was written by Bill Milliken in 1968. His book came out of his experience as a youth worker in the tough, Lower East Side of Manhattan in the late sixties. He attributes his ability to combine love with toughness to his faith in a loving God. This concept as developed by Milliken has a spiritual origin. Essentially, what Bill learned was that you need to love, in this case gang members, in spite of their behavior, but also to confront them when they made decisions and took actions that were wrong.

Over time, tough love has become associated with the addiction movement and the actions people need to take to prevent or intervene in drug usage situations. Tough love is the opposite of enabling, another term used in the addiction field. Resisting enabling behavior is tough love in action. In the context of a young adult who is resisting the change of moving toward more independence, not supporting such behavior but continuing to stay loving is tough love in action. Sometimes those who have been part of the tough love parenting movement have acted not out of love but out of frustration or who's in control. It's important to maintain a loving connection with your young adult even though you may be telling them they can't live at home or they can't have more money. Why? Because we as parents are wired to love our children and never lose that desire even though we may bury it in times of hurt and anger. The anger often masks the deeper emotion of rejection or hurt. Our young adults need to know that no matter what they are loved.

They need to know that the door of love is open to them even though the door to your house may not be.

There has been considerable research on tough love approaches to treating addicts, and there is evidence that harsh treatment within such programs for teens can be detrimental.

The matrix on page 64 illustrates these two dimensions of tough love—holding a young adult responsible and loving the young adult. I am borrowing and translating this approach to parenting from the work of Mark Murphy.[4] Murphy has studied leadership in business and found the top leaders—who he calls 100 Percenters—are very challenging but also connected and caring. I think the effective mix that makes up appropriate tough love involves similar elements. Appropriate tough love is the sweet spot of integrity and unconditional love. The goal is to be in the upper right quadrant demonstrating both high integrity and high love.

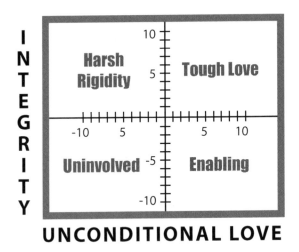

UNCONDITIONAL LOVE

Stages of Change

The saying: "Timing is everything" is true in trying to manage the dynamic of the letting go process with young adults. It is challenging for parents to discern when to move in with love and support and when to back off. This dance is about joining, synchronizing moves, and timing. When it comes to how much to let go and support autonomy, parents may have a different understanding of the timing compared to when they were young adults. Some young adults pull away too soon and may bounce back home. Others seem to have a hard time moving out. So it's important to use language that can match the young adult's stage of moving toward independence.

James Prochaska developed a model of change in 1977, and he and his colleagues have researched and applied this model to a number of different change opportunities beginning with smoking cessation. He proposes a model that identifies six stages people go through to undertake a change, whether that involves breaking an old habit or starting something new (see bibliography on page 79). The stages and the likely position of the young adult in the process of moving toward mature independence are described on the next page.

Stage I: Precontemplation. At this stage the young adult isn't giving much thought if any to moving out and on in their life. They may be enjoying their current status and feel no need to contemplate a change.

Stage II: Contemplation. At this stage the young adult is recognizing that their current status is not sustainable, and they may need to consider making a change someday. There is a recognition that the young adult may need to make some changes in the future.

Stage III: Preparation. At this stage the young adult is clearly intending to take actions that would enable them to move to a different place—independence, new identity, intimate relations. There is also recognition that the current status is unsustainable: Can't live at home the rest of my life. Can't continue to deliver pizzas for the rest of my life. At this stage the young adult may set a date to move out or start school.

Stage IV: Action. This is the stage at which the young adult begins to make progress in addressing the tasks of this developmental stage—moves out, gets a job, starts an intimate relationship. So there is clear lift off from the launch pad.

Stage V: Maintenance. This is the stage at which the young adult persists and makes continued progress on the changes to which they have committed and overcomes obstacles that might interfere. They resist moving back home or asking for help from their parents.

Stage VI: Termination. The young adult has achieved the state of mature independence and has faced and overcome obstacles that may have interfered with this accomplishment. This achievement may occur at eighteen or thirty-five; some adults may struggle with this the rest of their lives. Termination does not mean the end of the relationship but the end of dependency.

How is this model helpful to parents of young adults? The model highlights the fact that movement or "change" to mature adulthood is dynamic and not something that just happens one day. It helps to be able to identify where the young adult is on the stages of change continuum. If they are at the precontemplative stage, it may be impossible to get them to consider the advantages of moving out and on. At the contemplative stage, parents can engage the young adult in envisioning a future—where might they live and what might they be doing. At the preparation stage, parents can partner with the young adult to help them set some change dates and identify the steps necessary to move forward in their lives. At the action stage, the parents can pitch in and help with the move, offer support for living away from home, and be available to coach and consult. At the maintenance stage, parents need to stay connected and support any and all actions that demonstrate positive movement on the developmental tasks. Finally, at the termination stage, parents and their adult children can enjoy their separateness and reinforce this while maintaining a loving connection. This is the subject of the sixth book in this series - *Growing Apart: Letting Go of Our Young Adults.*

For people to change, they must have a growing awareness of the benefits of the change and the drawbacks of not changing, the confidence they can change, and ideas about how to navigate the path forward. Parents can be great coaches and consultants in this process while recognizing they need to time and match their words and actions to their young adult's stage of change.

Solutions Versus Problem Approach

> *"One cannot teach a man anything.*
> *One can only enable him to learn from within."*
> —Galileo

When you no longer have the power to direct another person, as you have had in the past with your children, how do you continue to engage them in ways that might influence their behavior? One of the common recurrent patterns in parent adolescent/young adult relationships is the conflict over the parent wanting to direct, control, or fix the young adult and the young adult resisting and wanting to make their own decisions. Often arguments occur around money, parental style, young adult relationships, careers, and jobs. Many times the arguments gravitate to problems, past behavior, and blaming. One way to break this pattern is to take a solutions approach versus a problem approach. This is a concept that grew out of the brief therapy movement and has been applied in business settings and to a limited extent in parent-child relationships. In this approach, picture sitting around the kitchen table with your young adult discussing their challenges and together generating possible solutions. Be sure to keep responsibility on your young adult to both come up with solutions and ultimately choose solutions. Your role is a collaborator working with your young adult to generate solutions. The problem may be identifying a process and steps to attain mature independence. This "coaching" (see earlier reference to coaching) approach assumes:

- Underlying developmental tasks of identity, independence, intimacy, and a need to find happiness drives decisions and actions. This assumes positive, underlying intent.

- Focusing on solutions versus problems moves away from the past and who is to blame to the future and how to solve the problem.

- Focusing on solutions reduces resistance, more effectively engages the young adult, and fosters more of a partnering approach to issues.

- The solutions exist in your young adult's mind, and the young adult has the resources and strengths to implement these.

- The past cannot be changed but the future can be influenced and created.

- The goal is to uncover or elicit the unique solutions that will be supported and implemented by the young adult.

If you focus on problems, you become an expert on problems. If you focus on solutions, you become an expert on solutions.

Skills necessary to use a solutions approach

1. Use effective listening skills and listen for both what the young adult is saying and their feelings. If you need to hone your skills in listening and enquiry, review the book *Can You Speak Millennial "ese?"* available at www.parentslettinggo.com.

2. Use effective enquiry skills by asking open-ended questions that require more than a yes-no response to draw out the young adult's thinking and solutions. Here are some examples: What ideas do you have as to how to solve . . .? What have you tried in the past that might work with this problem? What do you think your best friend might suggest to solve it? What do you see as the pros and cons of different options?

3. Use a scaling question. An example would be: What confidence do you have that you will move out in six months? Have your young adult rate their confidence on a 0-10 scale with 0 being no confidence and 10 being absolute confidence. They will typically pick a number between 4 and 8. Once they state a number ask them what factors are contributing to their confidence number. Affirm these answers. Then ask what could they do to raise their confidence to the next number and affirm these answers. Then ask if there is anything you can do to help raise the confidence level.

4. Use a collaborative approach when the issue involves both parents and the young adult. In such a case both parties have to first practice good listening and then generate possible solutions that might work for both. Use a problem solving approach where you throw out different solutions and then pick the best one or combination.

5. Be willing to compromise, allow the young adult to contribute ideas, and then invest in the solution and be willing to live with it even if may not be your preferred solution. When a young adult comes up with a solution, they are much more likely to invest in it than if a parent tells them the solution.

6. Change problems to goals. Most conflicts arise around issues of identity, independence, intimacy, and the young adult's efforts to find happiness. Keeping this in mind, convert the problem to a goal that can incorporate one or more of these developmental goals. Here are some examples. 1) Young adult: "I want to go to community college and not the university." Parent: "You want the freedom to choose where you go to school?" In this case, a smart parent would likely go along with this because it's cheaper for your young adult to go to community college. 2) Young adult: "I going to date this girl even though you don't like her." Parent: "You want to make your own decisions about who you date and you want us to support this? What ideas do you have that could help us get to know this girl and be more comfortable with her?" 3) Young adult: "I need to smoke weed because it relaxes me, and I have a lot of stress." Parent: "So I wonder if there are other approaches that you could try apart from smoking weed that might help you reduce your stress?"

Summary of Different Approaches to Influence

This section is a summary of the skills or techniques of influence from the different schools of thought described above. Your intent in using these skills is critical and must reflect your desire to listen, learn, love, and support the young adult and allow for them to make their own decisions and live with the consequences. Be transparent in your use of these techniques (as ways you have learned from this book) to help them move toward mature independence. They are techniques to help with interaction and support of your young adult and need to be used in that spirit and not as a method to manipulate or get them to do what you want them to do. The goal is to bring both love and backbone to their lives that help them move toward mature independence.

1. One can draw from one's childhood experiences but understand some things may not apply. Critically evaluate what worked with you and how this may or may not apply to a different young adult in a different time and circumstances. Be thoughtful. Don't just default to the parental autopilot in your head.

2. Be willing to say no in love if it will ultimately be best for the young adult and their well being. If angry or frustrated, take time to think if your behavior is in the upper-right quadrant of the Tough Love model described on page 64 or one of the other quadrants.

3. Take a staged approach to working with your young adult and influencing them on decisions they need to make. Are they still contemplating a decision? Ready to make a decision? Have made a decision? Your response and actions will be different depending on where they are on the stages of change.

4. Ask open-ended and evocative questions as described under the solutions oriented approach. Use scaling techniques to learn what's working and what they could do to increase their confidence of attainment of goals.

5. Avoid a problem focus and assigning blame that will trigger a defensive reaction. Approach a challenge in a collaborative manner where you and the young adult focus on generating solutions; have your young adult evaluate them and choose one that will work best.

6. Change problems to goals and reinforce and affirm positive talk regarding changes that will enable the young adult to reach goals.

7. All approaches require and start with a commitment by the parents to listen and understand what the young adult is saying and what need they may be trying to address.

> *"Grant that I may not so much seek to be consoled as to console, to be understood as to understand, to be loved as to love."*
> —Saint Francis of Assisi

CHAPTER 9

How Do I Take Care of Myself?

You are not alone.

In my experience, parents dealing with teens and young adults who are out of control or pursuing self-destructive ends are the most stressed and emotionally distraught people I know. The element that makes this particularly disturbing and frightening is the loss of control over the actions of your child. We have to come to grips with the

reality that at a certain point in time we no longer can control or direct the decisions and actions of our late adolescents and young adults. At best we can think about influencing and at worst we may be shut out completely by them. The good news is that you are not alone. As I have pursued developing materials for parents who are struggling with the launching process, I am amazed at how many folks have said, "Wow, we really need this help." And when I have held workshops on this subject, one of the highest-rated components is sharing with other parents and finding out you are not the only one struggling to launch a young adult.

How Parents Can Take Care of Themselves

- Strengthen the practices that enable parents to let go and give the young adult the best chance to launch without unresolved family attachments and expectations. These practices are part of the books in this series and include understanding, unconditional love, apology, forgiveness, integrity, and letting go.

- We need to embrace the assumptions stated at the outset of this book (page 3). We need to practice living out these assumptions, particularly the one that we cannot control our young adults and are not responsible for their actions.

- If you are in a two-parent family, the most critical action you can take is to ensure that you are on the same page, meaning that you work out differences in setting limits and showing love and support. You can't split these between the parents or the outcome can be disastrous for both the parents and the young adult. A specific action you can take is to commit to being a team and find the win-win and compromises in different approaches. Into their approaches, each parent needs to incorporate clear values and expectations along with active efforts to show love and support. If you tend to gravitate to one or the other side of these two actions, you need to increase your efforts to balance your approach. As an experiment—to learn about the side of tough love you are not exhibiting—I have had parents change roles for a week or two and then discuss the results. If dad was the tough guy, he becomes the accepting nurturing parent and the mom takes on the tough role. Each parent needs to exhibit both toughness and support. Young adults need to experience consistency in the parent's approach to them and know that each parent is capable of being firm and loving. Avoid inconsistency either between the parents or within each parent.

- Take care of yourself first. Find ways to detach and de-stress from the problems you are facing with your young adult. Don't churn about things 24-7. Set up a time to discuss with spouse or friend and save ideas or concerns for those discussion times. In other words, segment your talk time on the issues with your young adult. To reduce stress increase your physical exercise, get away, get out with friends, and take up a hobby that gives you pleasure and temporary escape from obsessing about your young adult. There's a reason why the airlines instruct adult passengers, in the event of an emergency, to put their oxygen mask on first and then put the child's mask on. Can you imagine trying to put the mask on your child without your mask on and the child resisting, pushing it away, and refusing your help? Eventually you both will pass out or die because neither of you put on the oxygen mask. With your mask on, you will survive and are much more likely to be able to influence your young adult to take action.

- Find other parents, family members, or friends you can talk with to vent and get ideas of what you can do. Seek help and ideas not only as to how you might approach your young adult but also how you can best take care of yourself. Social support is a huge factor in warding off depression.

Seek professional help if you can't seem to get on top of your anxiety or worries about your young adult. It's not an admission of defeat but a show of openness and strength to seek professional help. My guess is you may have suggested this to your young adult and encouraged this. Why shouldn't you practice what you preach? In many instances the parents are more distraught than the young adult and therefore better candidates for benefiting from professional help.

CHAPTER 10

Keepers

At the end of each of the six practice books I have identified some keepers or takeaways for your consideration. These keepers are my key points or reminders from this book. You may have your own list of reminders and that's great.

1. Understand young adults' actions, whether problematic or not, are driven by needs for identity, independence, and intimacy. A need for purpose and a desire for happiness also can be major drivers of behavior.

2. Take the time to listen and inquire to sincerely seek understanding versus tell and criticize or direct and control. Not listening is the number one complaint I hear from adolescents and young adults, and it is a skill that can be mastered. Be a great listener.

3. Express unconditional love and separate this from conditional approval for actions.

4. Practice apology, forgiveness, and compassion while holding firm to your values and requirements.

5. Demonstrate integrity that your young adult can count on: keeping promises, being clear about expectations, and following through.

6. Approach your young adult with an understanding of their stage of change and an understanding that "this too shall pass." They will not always be the way they are today. Be patient.

7. Approach your young adult in the spirit of seeking solutions and options versus focusing on the problem and what's wrong.

8. Commit to being firm, loving, and consistent both individually and as a couple.

9. Pick your battles and follow effective conflict management guidelines even if your young adult doesn't.

10. Ensure that your decisions and actions are driven by love and what's right, and not fear, anger, guilt, or need to avoid conflict and please your young adult.

Call to Action

This book is intended to help you evaluate your current thinking and actions related to your young adult and supporting their path to mature independence. The quizzes earlier in the book should help you identify areas that you might need to address. The value of this book is not in the reading but in applying what you have learned in a way that makes a positive difference in your parenting and relationship to  your young adult. Here are some questions to guide you. If you don't do something to move forward with what you have read and learned in the next twenty-four hours, you are likely not to apply anything.

1. Are there one or two behaviors or beliefs that are enabling (pages 15–16) that I need to address? What actions will I take to address these?

2. Is there one personal quality that demonstrates backbone (pages 11–13) that I will strengthen? How will I do this?

3. Are there one or two areas of the backbone readiness quiz (pages 19–20) that I need to address? What actions will I take to address these?

4. Is there one or more of the keepers listed previously that I would like address? How will I address this keeper?

5. What was the most important learning from this book, and how will I apply this to the parenting of my young adult?

6. What are the specific actions I will take to ensure that I have the support of family members, friends, or professionals?

7. What one or two actions am I willing to take in the next twenty-four hours that will help me start the process of applying what I have learned and begin to make the changes I need to make to be a more effective parent to my young adult?

NOTES

1. Michael Josephson. Personal communication February 8, 2018.

2. https://www.merriam-webster.com/dictionary/backbone.

3. Jeffrey Jensen Arnett and Joseph Schwab, "The Clark University Poll of Parents of Emerging Adults," Clark University, Worcester, MA, September 2013.

4. Mark Murphy, *Hundred Percenters: Challenge Your Employees to Give It Their All, and They'll Give You Even More*. New York: McGraw Hill, 2009.

Coleman, Joshua. *When Parents Hurt: Compassionate Strategies When You and Your Grown Child Don't Get Along.* New York: William Morrow, 2008.

Gottman, John and Nan Silver. *The Seven Principles for Making a Marriage Work.* New York: Harmony Books, 2015.

Milliken, Bill. *Tough Love.* Old Tappan, NJ: Fleming H. Revell Company, 1968.

Prochaska, James O., John C. Norcross, and Carlo C. Diclemente. *Changing for Good.* New York: Harper Collins Paperback, 2006.

Stoltzfus, Jack *Apology: The Gift We Give Our Young Adults.* Available at parentslettinggo.com and Amazon.com.

Stoltzfus, Jack. *Can You Speak Millennial "ese"? How to Understand and Communicate with Your Young Adult.* Available at parentslettinggo.com and Amazon.com.

Stoltzfus, Jack. *Forgiveness: The Gift We Share with Our Young Adults and Ourselves.* Available at parentslettinggo.com and Amazon.com.

Stoltzfus, Jack. *Love to Let Go: Loving Our Kids into Adulthood.* Available at parentslettinggo.com and Amazon.com.

Young, Joel L. and Christine Adamec. *When Your Adult Child Breaks Your Heart: Coping with Mental Illness, Substance Abuse, and the Problems That Tear Families Apart.* Guilford, CT: Lyons Press, 2013.

Resources to Address Enabling Behavior by Parents

Brown, Ann. *Backbone Power: The Science of Saying No.* Copyright©
Ann H. Brown, 2013.

Cloud, Henry and John Townsend, *Boundaries: When to Say Yes,
How to Say No to Take Control of Your Life.* Grand Rapids, MI:
Zondervan, 1992.

Isay, Jane. *Walking on Eggshells: Navigating the Delicate Relationship Between Adult Children and Parents.* New York: Anchor Books, 2007.

Katherine, Anne. *Where to Draw the Line: How to Set Healthy Boundaries Every Day.* New York: Fireside, 2000.

Levine, Madeline. *The Price of Privilege: How Parental Pressure and
Material Advantage Are Creating a Generation of Disconnected
and Unhappy Kids.* New York: Harper, 2006.

Nemzoff, Ruth. *Don't Bite Your Tongue: How to Foster Rewarding
Relationships with Your Adult Children.* New York: Palgrave Macmillan, 2008.

Stockman, Larry V. and Cynthia S. Graves, *Grown-up Children Who
Won't Grow Up.* Rocklin, CA: Prima Publishing, 1994.

,

Made in United States
Orlando, FL
24 April 2023

32419012R00050